T0418443

Hit It!

Consultants

Ashley Bishop, Ed.D.

Sue Bishop, M.E.D.

Publishing Credits

Dona Herweck Rice, *Editor-in-Chief*

Robin Erickson, *Production Director*

Lee Aucoin, *Creative Director*

Tim J. Bradley, *Illustrator Manager*

Janelle Bell-Martin, *Illustrator*

Sharon Coan, *Project Manager*

Jamey Acosta, *Editor*

Rachelle Cracchiolo, M.A.Ed., *Publisher*

Teacher Created Materials

5301 Oceanus Drive

Huntington Beach, CA 92649-1030

http://www.tcmpub.com

ISBN 978-1-4333-2932-6

© 2012 Teacher Created Materials, Inc.

Printed in Malaysia. THU001.50393

hit

I got a hit.

mitt

I have a mitt.

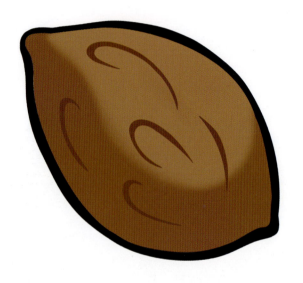

pit

I have a pit.

bit

I got bit!

Get the kit!

Glossary

bit

hit

kit

mitt

pit

Sight Words

**I   got
a   have
Get   the**

Extension Activities

Read the story together with your child. Use the discussion questions before, during, and after your reading to deepen your child's understanding of the story and the rime (word family) that is introduced.

The activities provide fun ideas for continuing the conversation about the story and the vocabulary that is introduced. They will help your child make personal connections to the story and use the vocabulary to describe prior experiences.

Discussion Questions
- Why do the girls in the story need the kit?
- What do we do to prevent bug bites?
- What can we use a mitt for at home?
- How would you feel if you got a hit in a ball game? Why?

Activities at Home
- If you have a first aid kit at home, find it with your child and talk about the contents of your kit. If you don't have a first aid kit, consider making one with your child. Discuss the types of items that you would put in a first aid kit and the importance of having one.
- Work with your child to locate foods in the kitchen that have a pit. Look closely at the pit with your child, and talk about what a pit is and why it is inside some types of fruit.